THE ROYAL HORTICULTURAL SOCIETY
ADDRESS BOOK

Commentary by Brent Elliott
Illustrations from
the Royal Horticultural Society's Lindley Library

FRANCES LINCOLN

Frances Lincoln Limited
4 Torriano Mews
Torriano Avenue
London NW5 2RZ
www.franceslincoln.com

The Royal Horticultural Society Address Book 2006
Copyright © Frances Lincoln Limited 2005

FRONT COVER
'Othonna, nov.sp. – a newly introduced South African composite', probably *Euryops laxus*, an unpublished
original drawing by Sydenham Teast Edwards.

BACK COVER
Narcissus poeticus, an unpublished original drawing by Sydenham Teast Edwards, dated Salisbury, 17 May.

TITLE PAGE
Helianthemum nummularium, an unpublished original drawing by John Curtis, dated January 1823.

INTRODUCTION

William Curtis was born in Alton, Hampshire, in 1746. From 1772 to 1777 he worked at the Chelsea Physic Garden before establishing his own botanic garden in Lambeth Marsh. In 1789 he started a nursery in Brompton, which moved to Chelsea after his death in 1799 and continued to trade until 1823. His most important works were the *Flora Londinensis* (1777–98) and the *Botanical Magazine*.

Founded in 1787, Curtis's *Botanical Magazine* has been published continuously ever since and is now the longest-running botanical periodical still in publication. For a decade, during which it passed its bicentenary, it went under the name of the *Kew Magazine*, but in 1995 it reverted, and it continues to appear as Curtis's *Botanical Magazine*, even though the Curtis family ceased to be connected with it in the 1830s. The format has stayed basically the same for over two centuries: plates presenting portraits of plants, with an accompanying leaf or leaves of text describing the plant in question. Until 1947 the plates were hand-coloured engravings, based on artists' original drawings; in that year the change to colour printing was made.

The most important of the early artists for the *Botanical Magazine* was Sydenham Teast Edwards (1768–1819). As few of the plates were signed before 1799, it is not known exactly how many plates he drew for the magazine, but he certainly illustrated most of the first forty-two volumes, which contain more than 1,700 plates. In 1815, Edwards left to found his own rival magazine, the *Botanical Register*, and thereafter his name disappeared from the *Botanical Magazine*, though in fact the magazine continued for some time to publish drawings he had completed before he left. Among the RHS's collection of Edwards' drawings are originals for coloured engravings published in the *Botanical Magazine* after his defection, but with the artist's name not provided in the published version.

After Edwards, two decades were to pass before there was a single dominant artist in the magazine (Walter Hood Fitch, who started in 1834 and made over 2,700 plates). In the interim John Curtis (1791–1862) – no relation to William – was probably the most important artist, responsible for some four hundred plates. James Sowerby (1757–1822) drew nearly a hundred, and at least nine were the work of Charles M. Curtis, John's brother (c.1795–1839). The RHS Lindley Library has a collection of drawings by all four of these artists, some of which are original drawings for the *Botanical Magazine*. A selection of these drawings, together with engravings from the early volumes of the magazine, illustrates this address book.

Brent Elliott
The Royal Horticultural Society

NOTE:—

DVD's SHOWN :—

Papaver rhoeas, an unpublished original drawing by John Curtis,
dated June 1824 and annotated by him 'from Mexican seeds but probably from Europe'.

A

ALBINONI ♦
  ADAGIO for ORGAN & STRINGS

ANTHEMS from KING'S
  CHOIR of KING'S COLLEGE CAMBRIDGE

AMICI DEFINED

♦ SEE UNDER PACHELBEL

Protea grandiflora, an unpublished original drawing by Sydenham Teast Edwards, dated 1 June, drawn from a specimen in the garden of John Alexander Woodford of Belmont House, Vauxhall.

A

J. S. BACH
CHRISTMAS ORATORIO

COLLECTION of VARIOUS PIECE

VIOLIN CONCERTOS in A & E

AS ABOVE BUT JEHUDI MENUHI
SUITE Nº 3 in Dº

BERLIN CONCERT, DOMINGO, NETREBKO
& VILLAZON

CHACONNE FROM PARTITA Nº 2 in D.

JANET BAKER WITH GERALD MOORE
VARIOUS PIECES.

BAROQUE VARIOUS CLASSIC FM

BARBER KORNGOLD & WALTON
VIOLIN CONCERTOS.

BACH FANTASIA & FUGEU in C.
" ORCHESTRAL SUITE Nº 3

BARBER

ADAGIO, VIOLIN CELLO CONCERTOS
§ SEE UNDER PACHELBEL

B

BRAHMS.
DOUBLE CONCERTO   #
CLARINET TRIO
HORN   TRIO
PIANO CONCERTO Nº2
VIOLIN "   " IN D.
ACADEMIC OVERTURE ✓
VARIATIONS of THEME by HAYDN
LULLABY (WIEGENLIED)
HUNGARIAN DANCES
 PIANO QUINTET
 SYMPHONY 1, 2, 3, 4
 TRAGIC OVERTURE
BRUCH
   VIOLIN CONCERTOS 1 & 3

BRUCKNER
   SYMPHONY Nº2
   "   "   " Nº5
         Nº4 ROMANTIC

BEETHOVEN

PIANO CONCERTOS N°s 4 & 5

✱ TRIPLE CONCERTO N° 1 2 RECORDINGS

SYMPHONIES N° 5

PIANO SONATAS 14, 3, 5, 8

STRING QUARTET N° 10

TRIO "GHOST" N° 70

CORIOLAN OVERTUE OP 62

FIDELIO OVERTURE OP 72

EGMONT OVERTURE

EROICA SYMPHONY

SYMPHONY N° 9

SYMPHONY N° 3

} CLASSIC FM

PTO

B

BORODIN # SEE UNDER MUSSORGSKY

NIGHT on BARE MOUNTAIN

POLOVTSIAN DANCES

IN STEPPES of CENTRAL ASIA
STRING QUARTETS I & II

BOCCHERINI,
    MINUET φ

BORODIN

ROMANTIC RUSSIA
PRINCE IGOR OVERTURE
   "   "   POLOVTSIAN DANCES
SYMPHONY Nº2

BRITTEN, VIOLIN CONCERTO
  "   "   OVERTURE CANADIAN
                   CARNIVAL

BRITTEN & LENNOX BERKLEY
  SUITE of CATALAN DANCES

φ SEE UNDER PACHELBEL

C

CHOPIN
PIANO CONCERTOS N⁰ 1 & 2
COLLECTION of VARIOUS WORKS

COATES ERIC
VARIOUS MARCHES etc +
SAXO RHAPSODY

CHABRIER ESPAÑA *

C

CLASSIC FM CD'S

HALL of FAME VOL 1
" " VOL 2
CLASSICS ON TV
" " FILM
CHRISTMAS MUSIC (2)
" " JOY
" " PEACE
SMOOTH CLASSICS AT SEVEN
GREATEST OPERA CHORUSES
FAVOURITE BAROQUE
GREAT SYMPHONIES.
BEAUTY of the VIOLIN.
ROMANTIC CELLO
SERENITY.
~~BAROQUE~~

C

D

DVORÁK

PIANO CONCERTO IN G **

SYMPHONIES Nᵒˢ 8 & 9

PIANO QUINTETS in A &E ‡

PIANO TRIO "DUNKY" **

‡ SEE BRAHMS

** SEE SCHUBERT

Narcissus x odorus, an unpublished original drawing by Sydenham Teast Edwards.

D

D

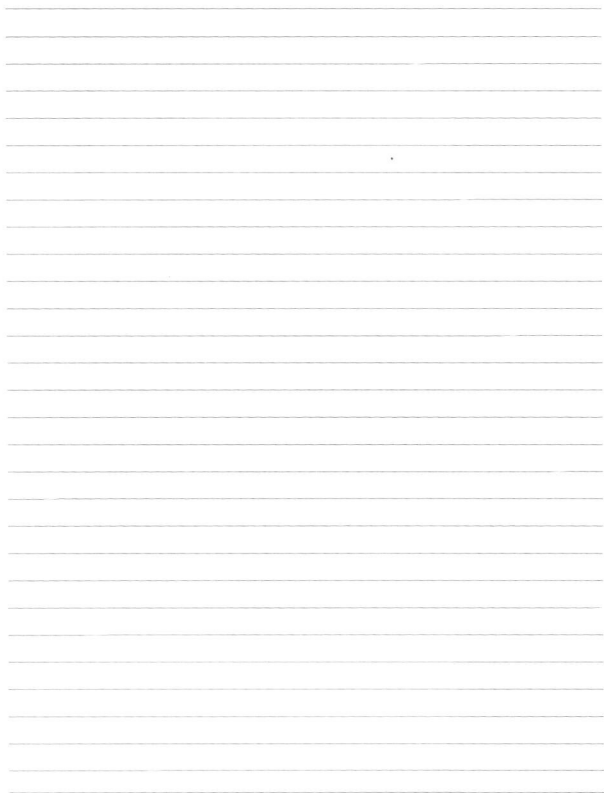

D

Narcissus poeticus, an unpublished original drawing by Sydenham Teast Edwards, dated Salisbury, 17 May.

E

ELGAR

VIOLIN CONCERTO KENNEDY

CELLO CONCERTO DU PRE

SYMPHONY N°2

    "   "   N°3

SEA PICTURES JANET BAKER

ENIGMA VARIATIONS ⎤

INTRODUCTION & ALLEGRO ⎪ ONE

COCKAIGNE   CD.

SERENADE for STRINGS ⎦

DREAM of GERONTIUS

SELECTION of VARIOUS (CLASSIC FM)

SEA PICTURES & THE

MUSIC MAKERS   SARAH
                CONNOLLY.

E

E

ELGAR SYPHONY Nº1
& ORGAN SONATAS

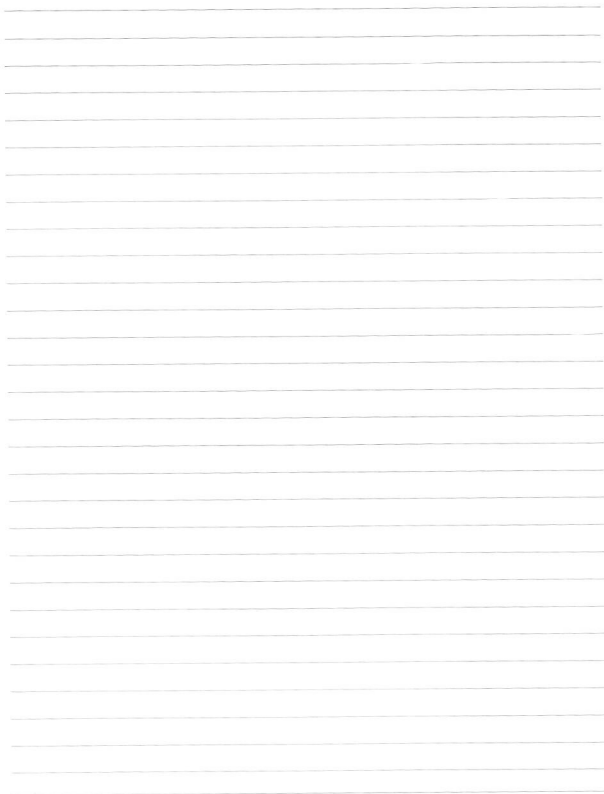

E

'*Magnolia purpurea*: purple magnolia', a hand-coloured engraving for plate 390 of Curtis's *Botanical Magazine*, published in November 1797. Although it is unsigned, the artist was probably Sydenham Teast Edwards.

F

FAURÉ
REQUIEM

JOHN FIELD PIANO SONATAS

Iris spuria subspecies *halophila*, an unpublished original drawing by John Curtis, dated June 1824.

F

F

F

'*Pyrus coronaria*: sweet-scented crab tree', an original drawing, dated 4 June, 1818, by Sydenham Teast Edwards for plate 2009 of Curtis's *Botanical Magazine*, published in September 1818.

Syd. Edwards del.

G

GRIEG
EXCERPTS - PEER GYNT, PIANO CON
LAST SPRING, HOLBERG, LYRIC &
BRIDAL PROCESSION etc   ONE
                         CD.

☨ GLINKA RUSLAN & LYUDMILA OVERTURE

SUSAN GRAHAM   ARIAS from GLUCK, MOZART

GLUCK.
   DANCE of THE BLESSED SPIRITS ☦

☨ SEE UNDER BORODIN ROMANTIC RUSSIA
☦ SEE UNDER PACHELBEL

Primula auricula 'Cockup's Eclipse', an unpublished original drawing by Sydenham Teast Edwards.   PTO

G

ANGELA GHEORGHIU & ROBERTO
ALAGNA. DRESDEN
"CLASSICS ON A SUMMER EVENING"

G

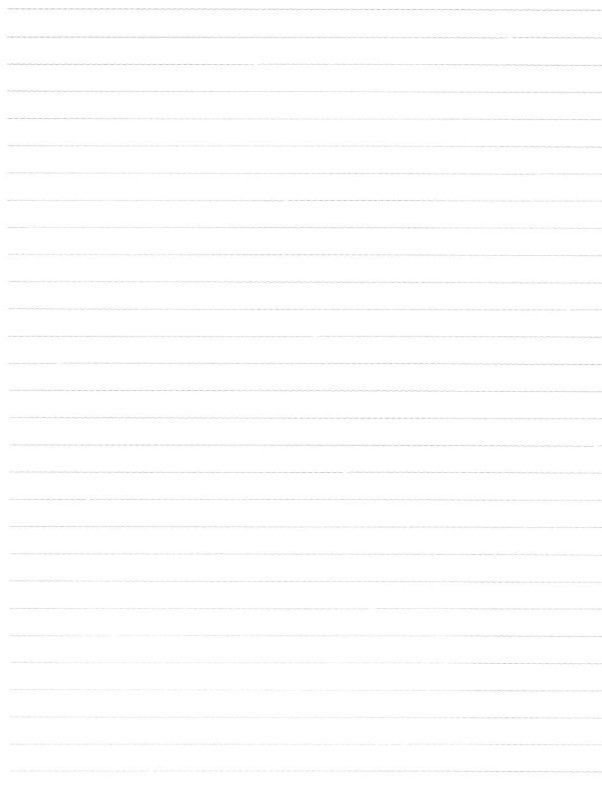

G

Rhododendron fragrans, an unpublished original drawing by John Curtis, dated June 1819.

H

HAYDN. MICHAEL & JOSEPH
CREATION (JOSEPH)
2 FLUTE CONCERTOS
SYMPHONY in F } MICHAEL
SYMPHONY N° 22 (JOSEPH
SYMPHONY N° 104 LONDON
SYMPHONY N° 94 SURPRISE
WIND QUARTET DIVERTIMENTO
(ST ANTONY CHORAL)

HANDEL
ROYAL FIREWORKS
QUEEN of SHEBA
ZADOK the PRIEST
HALLELUJAH CHORUS

Aconitum variegatum, an unpublished original drawing by James Sowerby, dated 3 August, 1819.

HOLST
THE PLANETS
THE MYSTIC TRUMPETER

HORNE MARILYN SINGS
FAMOUS ARIAS   DVD

HUMMEL
PIANO CONCERTO in B MINOR
PIANO CONCERTO in A MINOR

H

Rosa multiflora: bramble-flowered rose', an original drawing, dated 20 July, by Sydenham Teast Edwards for plate 1059 of Curtis's *Botanical Magazine*, published in October 1807 (with right-to-left reversal).

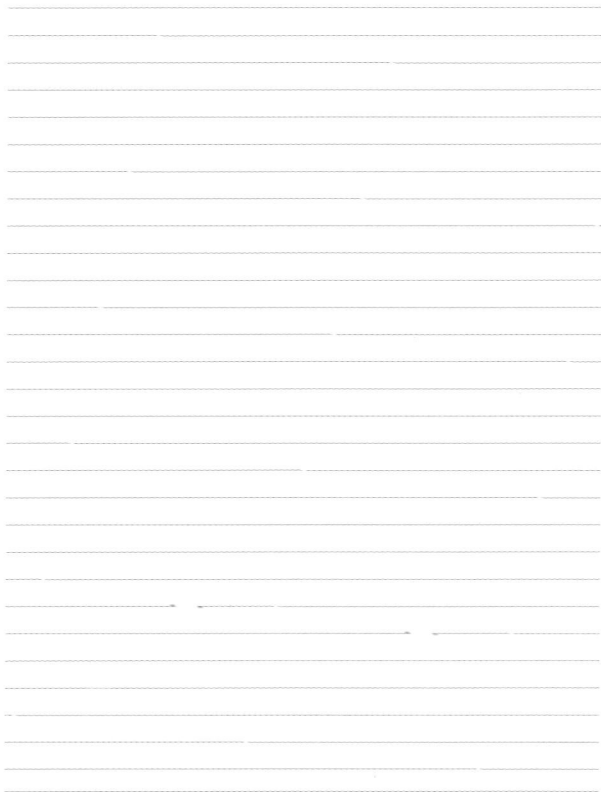

I

'*Amaryllis reginae*: Mexican lily', a hand-coloured engraving, signed by
Sydenham Teast Edwards, for plate 453 of Curtis's *Botanical Magazine*, published in August 1799.

I

J

JENKINS KATHERINE

LIVING A DREAM
SECOND NATURE

JANINE JANSEN VIOLINIST

PLAYS A SELECTION

'*Rosa lutea ß bicolour*: red and yellow Austrian rose', an original drawing, dated 23 June, by Sydenham Teast Edwards for plate 1077 of Curtis's *Botanical Magazine*, published in June 1818.

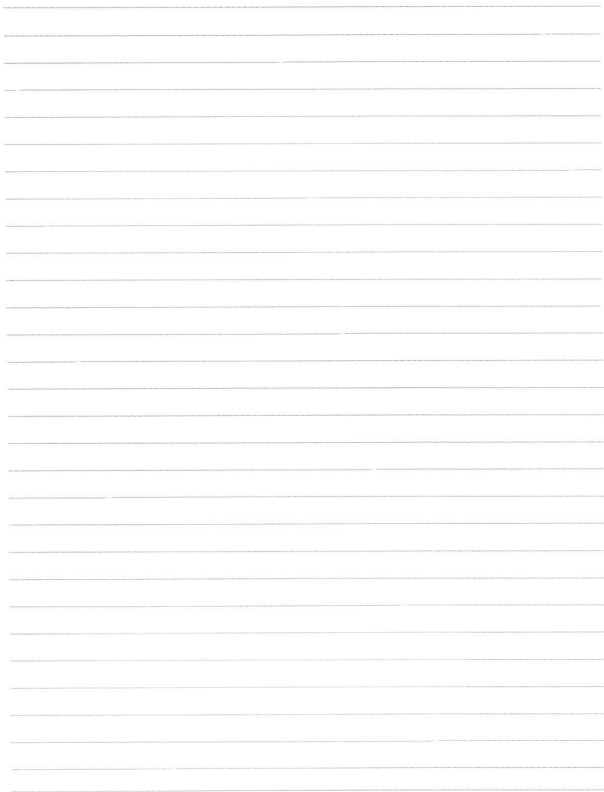

J

'*Centaurea montana*: greater blue bottle', a hand-coloured engraving for plate 77 of Curtis's *Botanical Magazine*, published in March 1789. There is no artist's signature.

K

KRAUS

SYMPHONY in C MINOR.

VIOLIN & ORCHESTRA in C MAJOR

FUNERAL SYMPHONY in C MINOR

KORNGOLD. E. VIOLIN CONCERTO
SEE UNDER BARBER

K

K

LISZT
LES PRÉLUDES
TASSO, LAMENTO e TRIONFO
PROMETHEUS

LEONCAVALLO
PAGLIACCI SEE MASCAGNI ⊗

LALO SYMPHONIE ESPAGNOLE
SEE SIBELIUS

'Lathyrus odoratus: sweet pea or vetchling', a hand-coloured engraving for plate 60 of Curtis's *Botanical Magazine*, published in August 1790. There is no artist's signature.

L

L

L

'*Begonia evansiana*: two-coloured begonia', an original drawing, dated 4 September, 1811,
by Sydenham Teast Edwards for plate 1473 of Curtis's *Botanical Magazine*, published in June 1812.

M

MOZART

CONCERTO for VIOLIN & ORCH Nᵒ4 in D K218

" " " " Nᵒ6 in E K268

RONDO CONCERTANTE VIOLIN B FLAT K269

" " " " in C K373

SONATAS for PIANO & VIOLIN K526 & 547

CORONATION MASS K317

MISSA SOLEMNIS in C MINOR K 139

PIANO CONCERTOS 19 & 23 K459 & 488

M

" " " " 21 (ELVIRA MADIGAN)

" " " " 24   SEE NEXT PAGE

SYMPHONIES 25, 29 & 33 K183, 201 & 319

" " 16, 18 & 25 K128, 130, 183

" " 38 & 41 K504 & 551

CASSATION in G   K63

HORN CONCERTOS etc BARRY TUCKWELL
PTO

'Catalpa syringifolia: common catalpa', an original drawing, dated 20 August, by Sydenham Teast Edwards for plate 1094 of Curtis's *Botanical Magazine*, published in March 1808 (with right-to-left reversal).

MAHLER

SYMPHONIES Nº 1

        "   "   Nº 2 RESURRECTION

        "   "   Nº 5 SIMON RATTLE

        "   "   Nº 9

KINDERTOTENLIEDER

MACDOWELL
PIANO CONCERTO Nº 2 ♦

MATT MONRO. SELECTION.

MIGNON by THOMAS. 3. CD'S
with MARILYN HORNE, RUTH WELTING usw

MOZART
SINFONIA CONCERTANTE K 364 ⎫ MAXIM
VIOLIN CONCERTO Nº 4 K 218 ⎬ VENGI
      "   "   Nº 2 K 211 ⎭
    MAXIM VENGEROV

❧ SEE UNDER SCHUMANN

MOZART

EINE KLEINE NACHTMUSIK K525

SALZBURG SYMPHONY N°1 K136

" " " " N°2 K137

" " " " N°3 K138

MOZART VARIOUS MASTERPIECES
  WITH BOOKLET.

CLASSIC FM. GREATEST MOZART
          SELECTIONS

PIANO CONCERTOS 19, 20, 21, 22 & 23
CLARINET QUINTET ⏀
SUSAN GRAHAM SINGS ARIAS

MASCAGNI
          CAVALLERIA RUSTICANA ⊛

MUSSORGSKY
      PICTURES at an EXHIBITION ‡‡
  * ⎱ KHOVANSCHCHINA PRELUDE
    ⎰ NIGHT ON THE BARE MOUNTAIN

                                    PTO

⊛ SEE LEONCAVALLO   ⏀ SEE SCHUBERT
‡‡ " BORODIN   * SEE UNDER BORODIN

M

MOZART MARRIAGE of FIGARO
ANNA NETREBKO
WIENER PHIL

N

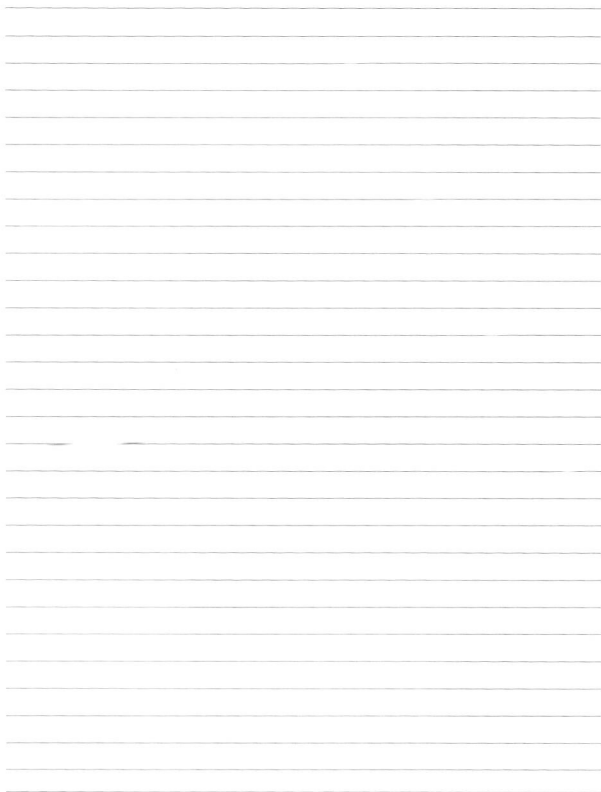

N

'*Hydrangea hortensis*: garden hydrangea', a hand-coloured engraving, signed by Sydenham Teast Edwards, for plate 438 of Curtis's *Botanical Magazine*, published in March 1799.

O

OPERA ALBUM
2 CD's of 19 ARIAS.

O

PQ

PACHEBEL♪
CANON

PROKOFIEV ROMEO & JULIET
SUITES 1 & 2

POPP LUCIA
2. CD's SELECTION of ARIAS.
INCL. & TATIANA LETTER. (EUGENE ONEGIN)✗

PURCELL HENRY
DIDO & AENEAS JANET BAKER
AYRES for the THEATRE
THE FAIRES of INSTRUMENTS
ESSENTIAL PURCELL THE KINGS CONSORT

SEE ALSO TSCHAIKOVSKY
SEE ALSO ALBINONI, BACH, VIVALDI, GLUCK &
BOCCHERINI.

'Plumbago capensis: phlox-like lead-wort', an original drawing, dated August 1819, by John Curtis for plate 2110 of Curtis's Botanical Magazine, published in November 1820.

PQ

R

RACHMANINOV

    PIANO CONCERTOS 2
                3 & 4
    "RHAPSODY" ON THEME of PAGANINI

    SYMPHONY N°2

RAVEL
    TZIGANE (SEE SIBELIUS)

RESPIGHI PINES of ROME

'Colchicum byzantinum: broad-leaved colchicum', a hand-coloured engraving, signed
by Sydenham Teast Edwards, for plate 1122 of Curtis's *Botanical Magazine*, published in July 1808.

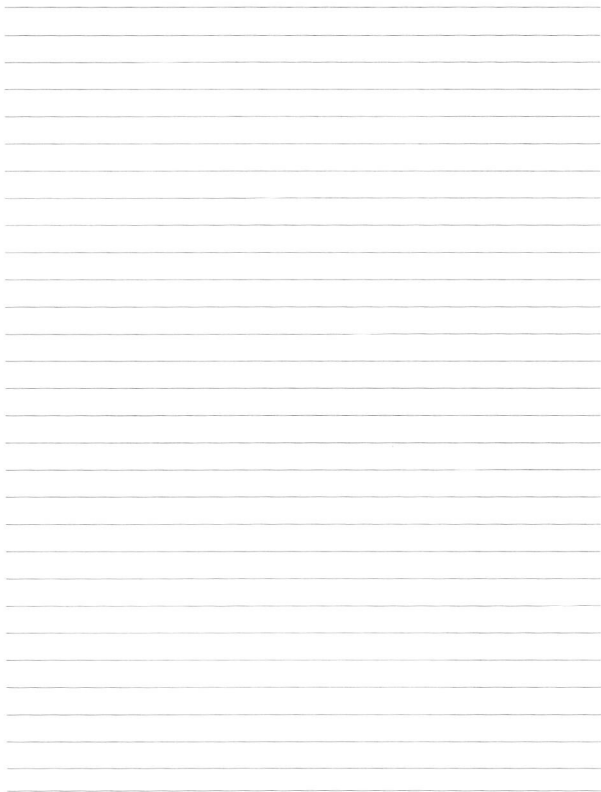

R

'Dahlia superflua: fertile-rayed dahlia', an original drawing by Sydenham Teast Edwards for plate 1885B of Curtis's *Botanical Magazine*, published in February 1817. There is no artist's signature.

S

SAINT-SAËNS
SYMPHONY 3 ORGAN
LE CARNAVAL des ANIMAUX
PIANO CONCERTO N°2
DANSE MACABRE.
VIOLIN CONCERTO N°3
} DOUBLE
} C.D.

CELLO CONCERTOS N°1 & 2
SUITE, OP 16.
ALLEGRO APPASSIONATO.
THE SWAN.

PIANO CONCERTOS N°2 & 4

~~TROUT~~ + ~~OTL~~

SCHUMANN
PIANO CONCERTO N° OP 54.
SYMPHONY N°2 BBC PHIL. BBC 2006 PROMS '96
SCHUBERT WANDERER FANTASY
SYMPHONIES N°3 & N°5 BB
TROUT.

SMETANA "MA VLAST"

S

S

SHOSTAKOVICH

SYMPHONY N°7 LENINGRAD

N°5 VINYL

S

SIBELIUS
    SYMPHONIES N^{0}5 & 6; 7

    VIOLIN CONCERTO

    EN SAGA

    N^{0}2 SJMPHONY

SMETANA.
    BARTERED BRIDE
    STRING QUARTET N^{0}1
    MEMORY of PILSEN

    MA VLAST.

STRAUSS RICHARD
    VIER LETZTE LIEDER
    JESSY NORMAN.

S

‘*Thunbergia alata*: winged-leaved thunbergia’, an original drawing, dated June 1825, by John Curtis for
plate 2592 of Curtis's *Botanical Magazine*, published in August 1825.

T

TCHAIKOVSKY.

SERENADE for STRINGS ✗

ANDANTE CANTABILE φ

PIANO CONCERTOS Nº 1 & 3

    "   "   2 & 3

    "   "   1 & 2

SYMPHONIES Nº 5

    "   MANFRED

    "   Nº 6 PATHETIQUE

✗   "   Nº 4

ROMEO & JULIET FANTASY OVERTURE

MARCH SLAV, CAPPRICIO ITALIEN,

1812, ROMEO & JULIET

✗ ROMEO & JULIET

OPERA EUGENE ONEGIN. VOL 1

    STRING QUARTETS Nº 1 & 2

    "   "   VOL 2

THOMAS opera MIGNON complete

work on 3 CD's SEE UNDER M.

                              T

TCHAIKOVSKY EUGENE ONEGIN

φ SEE UNDER SCHUBERT   ✗ SEE CHABRIER

'Symphoria racemosa: snowberry', an original drawing, dated July 1820,
by John Curtis for plate 2211 of Curtis's Botanical Magazine, published in February 1821.

T

'*Tritonia crispa*', an unpublished original drawing by Sydenham Teast Edwards, dated 24 May. It was drawn from a specimen in the *Turnham Green nursery* of Richard Williams.

U V

VIVALDI
CONCERTO for STRINGS & CONTINUO &
CLASSIC FM BEST of VIVALDI INCL
4 SEASONS, MANDOLIN CONCERTO, GLORIA etc
a TOTAL of 14.

VAUGHAN WILLIAMS.
GREENSLEEVES
THOMAS TALLIS   } ONE
NORFOLK RHAPSODY   } CD

LARK ASCENDING
GREEN SLEEVES
ENGLISH FOLK SONGS   ONE
THE WASPS   CD
NORFOLK RHAPSODY   HMV
THOMAS TALLIS   CLASIC
FIVE VARIANTS of 'DIVES & LAZARUS'

~~SEA SYMPHONY SYMPHONY Nº 1~~
SEA SYMPHONY Nº 1

U V

SEE UNDER PACHELBEL

P.T.O.

U V

VERDI. LA TRAVIATA
ANNA NETREBKO

'*Cornus mascula*: cornelian cherry', an original drawing, dated September 1823,
by John Curtis for plate 2675 of Curtis's *Botanical Magazine*, published in August 1826.

W

WALTON. W.
    VIOLIN CONCERTO in E ⎤ PHYLLIS SELLICK
    VIOLA   "   "   in A ⎬ CBS.
    SINFONIA CONCERTANTE. ⎦

    VIOLIN CONCERTO. BARBER &
    KORNGOLD SEE UNDER BARBER
    JAMES EHNES

WEBER
    DER FREISCHETZE OVERTURE
    CONCERTO for CLARINET.
    QUINTET for CLARINET in B.
    TURANDOT OVERTURE

W

'Helleborus niger: black hellebore, or Christmas rose', a hand-coloured engraving for
plate 8 of Curtis's Botanical Magazine, published in March 1786. There is no artist's signature.

W

_____

_____

_____

_____

_____

_____

_____

_____

_____

_____

_____

_____

_____

_____

_____

_____

_____

_____

_____

_____

_____

_____

_____

_____

_____

_____

X Y Z

X Y Z